ARCTIIDAE

600 Butterflies & Moths

IN FULL COLOR

W. F. Kirby

DOVER PUBLICATIONS, INC.
Mineola, New York

Introduction

Butterflies and moths belong to the order *Lepidoptera,* or scale-winged insects, which forms part of the class *Insecta,* the largest and most important division of the sub-kingdom *Articulata,* or jointed animals. The beautiful forms and colors of butterflies, the intricacy of their markings, and their graceful evolutions in the air and around flowers, have always caused them to be much admired by lovers of the beauties of nature. Almost every child has hunted butterflies through the woods and fields, or has reared silkworms or other moths, and been delighted to find the newly emerged insect in the box along with the empty pupa-case. Very often, just the remembrances of these youthful pleasures lead many to return to it in their mature years. The beauty and the wonderful transformations of butterflies and moths have attracted attention and pleased the fancy from the most ancient times. Philosophers have even reverently traced in them the symbol of the soul, and afterwards, of immortality; for there is a beautiful analogy between the graceful winged insect emerging from the dark, motionless pupa, and the spirit leaving its mortal body and winging its flight to higher regions.

W. F. KIRBY

Bibliographical Note

This Dover edition, first published in 2007, contains sixty-one full-color plates from *European Butterflies and Moths,* originally published by Cassell, Petter, Galpin & Co., London, in 1882. A complete list of the contents of the plates and an Alphabetical Index of Latin Names appear at the end of the book.

DOVER *Pictorial Archive* SERIES

Library of Congress Cataloging-in-Publication Data

Kirby, W. F. (William Forsell), 1844–1912.
    [European butterflies and moths]
    600 butterflies and moths in full color / W. F. Kirby.
        p. cm.
    Includes index.
    Originally published: European butterflies and moths. London : Cassell, Petter, Galpin & Co. 1882.
    ISBN-13: 978-0-486-46139-7
    ISBN-10: 0-486-46139-4
    1. Butterflies—Europe—Identification. 2. Moths—Europe—Identification. 3. Butterflies—Europe—Pictorial works. 4. Moths—Europe—Pictorial works. I. Title. II. Title: Six hundred butterflies and moths in full color.

QL555.A1K57 2007
595.78'9—dc22

2007021492

Manufactured in the United States of America
Dover Publications, Inc., 31 East 2nd Street, Mineola, N.Y. 11501

Plate 2 PAPILIONIDAE

Plate 4 Pieridae

NYMPHALIDAE **Plate 5**

Plate 6 NYMPHALIDAE

Plate 8 NYMPHALIDAE

Plate 10 NYMPHALIDAE; DANAIDAE

Plate 12   SATYRIDAE; LIBYTHEIDAE; ERYCINIDAE

Plate 14 Lycaenidae; Hesperiidae

Plate 16 SPHINGIDAE

Plate 18 SPHINGIDAE

Plate 20   Zygaenidae; Syntomidae

Plate 22 Liparidae; Notodontidae

Plate 24 Cossidae; Cochliopodidae; Hepialidae; Psychidae

Plate 26 Lasiocampidae

LASIOCAMPIDAE **Plate 27**

Plate 28 DREPANULIDAE; NOTODONTIDAE

Plate 30 Cymatophoridae; Acronyctidae

Plate 32 ORTHOSIDAE

Plate 34 Agrotidae; Hadenidae

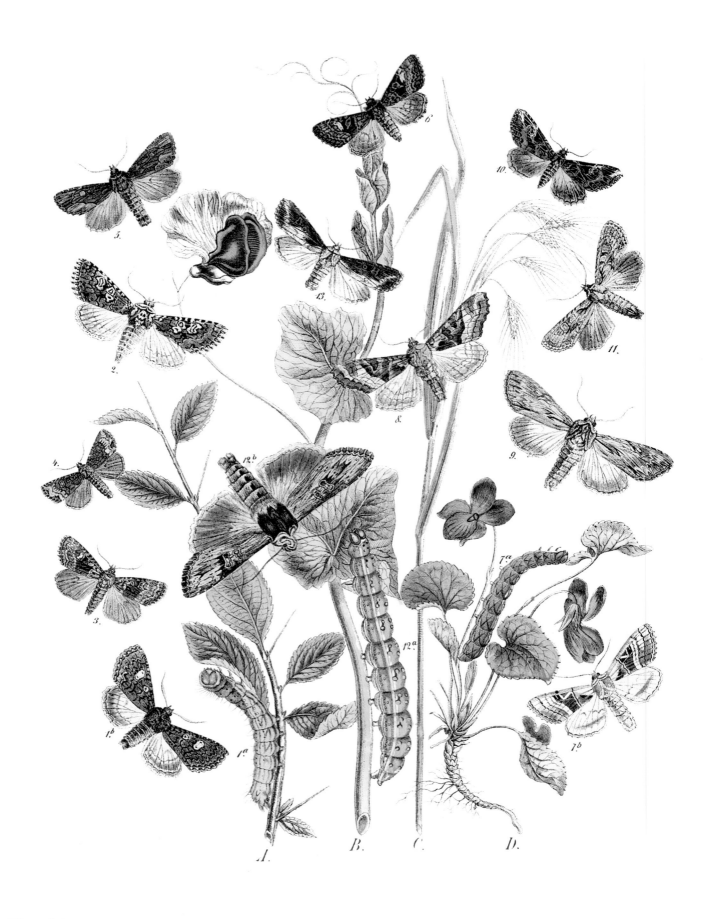

Plate 36 HADENIDAE; XYLINIDAE

Plate 38   PLUSIDAE; OPHIUSIDAE; TOXOCAMPIDAE

Plate 40   Noctuophalaenidae; Deltoidae; Chloephoridae

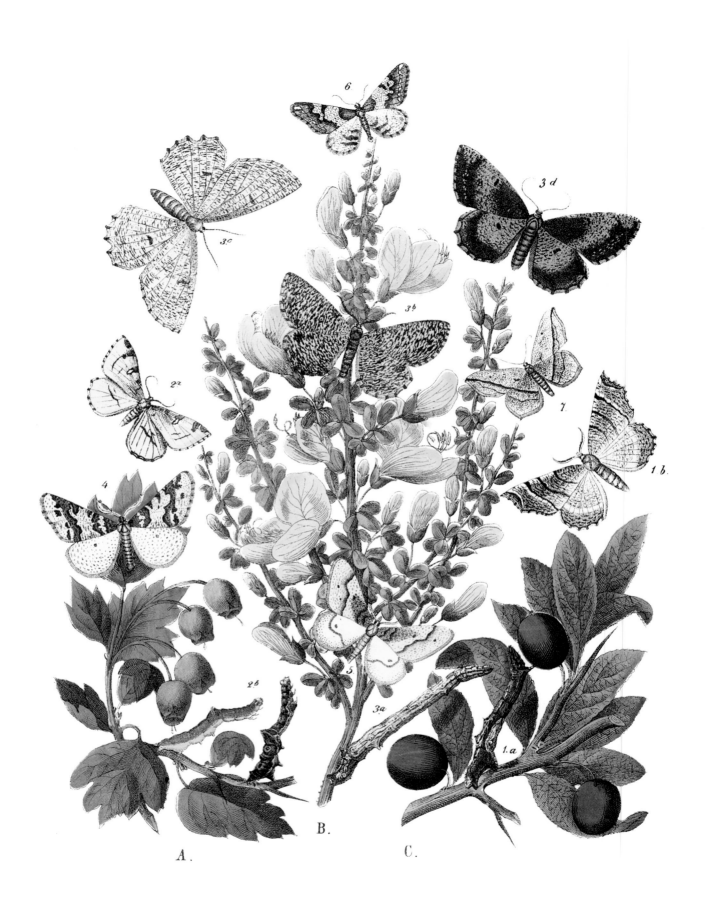

Plate 42 DENDROMETRIDAE

Plate 44 DENDROMETRIDAE

Plate 46 Phytometridae

Plate 48 Dendrometridae; Phytometridae

Plate 50 RHOPALOCERA

Plate 52 Noctuae

Plate 54 Noctuae

Plate 56 NOCTUAE; NYCTEOLIDAE

Plate 58 GEOMETRAE

Plate 60 TORTRICES; TINEAE; PTEROPHORI

EXPLANATION OF PLATES

Note: The plants figured are indicated by capital letters.

Frontispiece
ARCTIIDAE

Fig. 1, *a, b.*	*Callimorpha dominula*
Fig. 2, *a, b.*	*Callimorpha hera*
Fig. 3.	*Pieretes matronula*
Fig. 4.	*Nemeophila russula*
Fig. 5, *a–c.*	*Nemeophila plantaginis*
Fig. 6, *a–c.*	*Arctia caja*
Fig. 7.	*Arctia villica*
Fig. 8, *a, b.*	*Arctia purpurea*
Fig. 9.	*Arctia hebe*
Fig. 10.	*Spilosoma menthastri*
A. Ribwort Plantain	*Plantago lanceolata*
B. Bramble	*Rubus polymorphus*
C. Ground Ivy	*Glechoma hederacea*

Plate 1
PAPILIONIDAE

Fig. 1, *a–d.*	*Papilio podalirius*
Fig. 2.	*Papilio alexanor*
Fig. 3, *a–d.*	*Papilio machaon*
Fig. 4.	*Thais hypermnestra*
Fig. 5.	*Thais rumina*
Fig. 6.	*Doritis apollinus*
A. Blackthorn	*Prunus spinosa*
B. Caraway	*Carum carvi*

Plate 2
PAPILIONIDAE

Fig. 1, *a–d.*	*Parnassius apollo*
Fig. 2, *a, b.*	*Parnassius phoebus*
Fig. 3, *a–c.*	*Parnassius mnemosyne*
A. Orpine	*Sedum telephium*
B. Musk Thistle	*Carduus nutans*

Plate 3
PIERIDAE

Fig. 1, *a–c.*	*Leucophasia sinapis*
Fig. 2, *a–c.*	*Aporia crataegi*
Fig. 3, *a, b.*	*Pieris brassicae*
Fig. 4, *a, b.*	*Pieris rapae*
Fig. 5.	*Pieris napi*
Fig. 6.	*Pieris daplidice*
Fig. 7, *a, b.*	*Euchloe cardamines*
Fig. 8.	*Euchloe eupheno*
Fig. 9.	*Gonepteryx rhamni*
A. Trefoil	*Lotus siliquosus*
B. Rape	*Brassica napus*
C. Hawthorn	*Crataegus oxyacanthus*

Plate 4
PIERIDAE

Fig. 1.	*Colias palaeno*
Fig. 2.	*Colias phicomone*
Fig. 3, *a, b.*	*Colias hyale*
Fig. 4, *a–d.*	*Colias edusa*

A. Sainfoin	*Onobrychis sativa*
B.	*Coronilla varia*
C. Purple Clover	*Trifolium pratense*

Plate 5
NYMPHALIDAE

Fig. 1.	*Vanessa atalanta*
Fig. 2, *a–c.*	*Vanessa antiopa*
Fig. 3, *a–c.*	*Vanessa io*
Fig. 4.	*Vanessa urticae*
Fig. 5.	*Vanessa polychloros*
A. Birch	*Betula alba*
B. Stinging Nettle	*Urtica dioica*

Plate 6
NYMPHALIDAE

Fig. 1.	*Vanessa xanthomelas*
Fig. 2, *a–d.*	*Vanessa C-album*
Fig. 3, *a–d.*	*Vanessa cardui*
Fig. 4, *a, b.*	*Vanessa prorsa*
A. Spear Thistle	*Cirsium lanceolatum*
B. Stinging Nettle	*Urtica dioica*

Plate 7
NYMPHALIDAE

Fig. 1.	*Melitaea maturna*
Fig. 2.	*Melitaea cynthia*
Fig. 3, *a–d.*	*Melitaea aurinia*
Fig. 4.	*Melitaea didyma*
Fig. 5, *a–d.*	*Melitaea cinxia*
Fig. 6.	*Melitaea dictynna*
Fig. 7, *a–c.*	*Melitaea athalia*
Fig. 8, *a, b.*	*Argynnis aphirape*
A. Heath	*Calluna vulgaris*
B. Germander Speedwell	*Veronica chamaedrys*
C. Wild Heart's-ease	*Viola tricolor*
D. Scabious	*Scabiosa succisa*

Plate 8
NYMPHALIDAE

Fig. 1.	*Argynnis dia*
Fig. 2.	*Argynnis amathusia*
Fig. 3.	*Argynnis adippe*
Fig. 4, *a–d.*	*Argynnis aglaia*
Fig. 5.	*Argynnis lathonia*
Fig. 6, *a–d.*	*Argynnis paphia*
A. Wild Heart's-ease	*Viola tricolor*

Plate 9
NYMPHALIDAE

Fig. 1, *a, b.*	*Neptis lucilla*
Fig. 2, *a–e.*	*Limenitis sibylla*
A. Perfoliate Honeysuckle	*Lonicera caprifolium*
B. Common Honeysuckle	*Lonicera xylosteum*

Plate 10
NYMPHALIDAE—DANAIDAE

Fig. 1, *a–d.*   *Limenitis populi*
Fig. 2, *a–c.*   *Apatura iris*
Fig. 3.   *Apatura ilia, variety clytie*
Fig. 4.   *Charaxes jasius*
Fig. 5.   *Danaus chrysippus*
A. Aspen   *Populus tremula*
B. Sallow   *Salix caprea*

Plate 11
SATYRIDAE

Fig. 1, *a–c.*   *Hipparchia circe*
Fig. 2.   *Hipparchia hermione*
Fig. 3.   *Hipparchia briseis*
Fig. 4.   *Hipparchia cordula*
Fig. 5, *a–c.*   *Erebia medusa*
Fig. 6.   *Erebia epiphron*
Fig. 7.   *Erebia aethiops*
Fig. 8.   *Erebia ligea*
Fig. 9.   *Melanargia galathea*
Fig. 10.   *Satyrus aegeria*
A. Barren Brome   *Bromus sterilis*

Plate 12
SATYRIDAE—LIBYTHEIDAE—ERYCINIDAE

Fig. 1.   *Satyrus maera*
Fig. 2, *a–c.*   *Satyrus megaera*
Fig. 3.   *Epinephile hyperanthus*
Fig. 4, *a, b.*   *Epinephile janira*
Fig. 5.   *Epinephile tithonus*
Fig. 6.   *Coenonympha iphis*
Fig. 7, *a–c.*   *Coenonympha arcania*
Fig. 8.   *Coenonympha pamphilus*
Fig. 9.   *Libythea celtis*
Fig. 10.   *Nemeobius lucina*
A, D. Wood Poa   *Poa glauca*
B, C. Crested Dog's-tail Grass   *Cynosurus cristatus*

Plate 13
LYCAENIDAE

Fig. 1.   *Polyommatus euphemus*
Fig. 2, *a, b.*   *Polyommatus cyllarus*
Fig. 3.   *Polyommatus minima*
Fig. 4, *a, b.*   *Polyommatus argiolus*
Fig. 5.   *Polyommatus damon*
Fig. 6, *a–c.*   *Polyommatus corydon*
Fig. 7.   *Polyommatus bellargus*
Fig. 8, *a–d.*   *Polyommatus icarus*
Fig. 9.   *Polyommatus astrarche*
Fig. 10.   *Polyommatus argus*
Fig. 11.   *Polyommatus argiades*
Fig. 12.   *Lycaena hippothoe*
Fig. 13, *a, b.*   *Lycaena dispar,* variety *rutilus*
A.   *Coronilla varia*
B. Restharrow   *Ononis spinosa*
C. Whin   *Genista germanica*

Plate 14
LYCAENIDAE—HESPERIIDAE

Fig. 1, *a–c.*   *Lycaena virgaureae*
Fig. 2, *a, b.*   *Lycaena phlaeas*
Fig. 3.   *Thecla rubi*
Fig. 4, *a–c.*   *Thecla pruni*
Fig. 5, *a, b.*   *Zephyrus betulae*
Fig. 6.   *Zephyrus quercus*
Fig. 7, *a, b.*   *Spilothyrus alceae*
Fig. 8.   *Hesperia alveus*
Fig. 9.   *Hesperia malvae*
Fig. 10.   *Cyclopides morpheus*
Fig. 11.   *Cyclopides palaemon*
Fig. 12.   *Pamphila comma*
Fig. 13.   *Pamphila sylvanus*
Fig. 14.   *Pamphila thaumas*
A. Sheep's Sorrel   *Rumex acetosella*
B. Blackthorn   *Prunus spinosa*
C. Golden Rod   *Solidago virgaurea*
D. Dwarf Mallow   *Malva rotundifolia*

Plate 15
SPHINGIDAE

Fig. 1, *a–c.*   *Acherontia atropos*
Fig. 2.   *Choerocampa celerio*
Fig. 3, *a–c.*   *Choerocampa elpenor*
Fig. 4, *a, b.*   *Choerocampa porcellus*
A. Woody Nightshade   *Solanum dulcamara*
B. Yellow Bedstraw   *Galium verum*
C. Rose-bay, Willow-herb   *Epilobium angustifolium*

Plate 16
SPHINGIDAE

Fig. 1, *a, b.*   *Sphinx pinastri*
Fig. 2, *a, b.*   *Sphinx convolvuli*
Fig. 3, *a–c.*   *Sphinx ligustri*
A. Pine   *Pinus abies*
B. Privet   *Ligustrum vulgare*
C. Small Bindweed   *Convolvulus arvensis*

Plate 17
SPHINGIDAE

Fig. 1, *a, b.*   *Deilephila euphorbiae*
Fig. 2, *a, b.*   *Deilephila galii*
Fig. 3, *a–c.*   *Choerocampa nerii*
Fig. 4.   *Pterogon proserpina*
A. Oleander   *Nerium oleander*
B. White Bedstraw   *Galium mollugo*
C. Leafy-branched Spurge   *Euphorbia esula*

Plate 18
SPHINGIDAE

Fig. 1, *a–c.*   *Smerinthus tiliae*
Fig. 2.   *Smerinthus quercus*
Fig. 3, *a, b.*   *Smerinthus populi*
Fig. 4, *a, b.*   *Smerinthus ocellatus*
A. Apple   *Pyrus malus*
B. Poplar   *Populus pyramidalis*
C. Lime-tree   *Tilia parvifolia*

Plate 19
SPHINGIDAE—THYRIDIDAE—SESIIDAE

Fig. 1, *a–c.*	*Macroglossa stellatarum*	
Fig. 2.	*Macroglossa croatica*	
Fig. 3, *a–c.*	*Hemaris bombyliformis*	
Fig. 4.	*Hemaris fuciformis*	
Fig. 5.	*Thyris fenestrella*	
Fig. 6.	*Trochilium apiformis*	
Fig. 7.	*Trochilium crabroniformis*	
Fig. 8, *a, b.*	*Sesia tipuliformis*	
Fig. 9.	*Sesia conopiformis*	
Fig. 10.	*Sesia asiliformis*	
Fig. 11.	*Sesia culiciformis*	
Fig. 12.	*Sesia stomoxyformis*	
Fig. 13.	*Sesia formicaeformis*	
Fig. 14.	*Sesia empiformis*	
Fig. 15.	*Bembecia hylaeiformis*	
A. Red Currant	*Ribes rubrum*	
B. Common Honeysuckle	*Lonicera xylosteum*	
C. Goosegrass	*Galium aparine*	

Plate 20
ZYGAENIDAE—SYNTOMIDAE

Fig. 1.	*Aglaope infausta*
Fig. 2, *a, b.*	*Ino globulariae*
Fig. 3.	*Ino statices*
Fig. 4, *a, b.*	*Zygaena minos*
Fig. 5.	*Zygaena scabiosae*
Fig. 6.	*Zygaena achilleae*
Fig. 7, *a–c.*	*Zygaena lonicerae*
Fig. 8.	*Zygaena trifolii*
Fig. 9.	*Zygaena meliloti*
Fig. 10, *a, b.*	*Zygaena filipendulae*
Fig. 11, *a.*	*Zygaena ephialtes,* variety *coronillae*
Fig. 11, *b.*	*Zygaena ephialtes,* (type)
Fig. 11, *c.*	*Zygaena ephialtes,* variety *peucedani*
Fig. 12.	*Zygaena carniolica*
Fig. 13.	*Zygaena fausta*
Fig. 14.	*Zygaena laeta*
Fig. 15.	*Syntomis phegea*
A. Common Bird's-foot Trefoil	*Lotus corniculatus*
B. Mountain Trefoil	*Trifolium montanum*
C. Bush Vetch	*Vicia sepium*
D.	*Globularia vulgaris*

Plate 21
LITHOSIDAE—ARCTIIDAE

Fig. 1.	*Nudaria mundana*
Fig. 2, *a–c.*	*Calligenia miniata*
Fig. 3.	*Setina irrorella*
Fig. 4.	*Setina aurita*
Fig. 5.	*Setina aurita,* variety *ramosa*
Fig. 6.	*Setina mesomella*
Fig. 7.	*Lithosia deplana*
Fig. 8.	*Lithosia sororcula*
Fig. 9 (upper fig.)	*Lithosia complana*
Fig. 9, *a–c.*	*Oeonistis quadra*
Fig. 10.	*Gnophia rubricollis*
Fig. 11.	*Emydia striata*
Fig. 12, *a, b.*	*Deiopeia pulchella*
Fig. 13, *a, b.*	*Euchelia jacobaeae*

A. Lichen	*Parmelia stellaris*
B. Lichen	*Usnea florida*
C. Gromwell	*Pulmonaria officinalis*
D. Ragwort	*Senecio jacobaea*
E. Forget-me-not	*Myosotis palustris*

Plate 22
LIPARIDAE—NOTODONTIDAE

Fig. 1.	*Orgyia gonostigma*
Fig. 2, *a–c.*	*Orgyia antiqua*
Fig. 3.	*Dasychira selenitica*
Fig. 4, *a–c.*	*Dasychira fascelina*
Fig. 5, *a–c.*	*Dasychira pudibunda*
Fig. 6, *a, b.*	*Dasychira abietis*
Fig. 7, *a, b.*	*Cnethocampa processionea*
Fig. 8.	*Pygaera anachoreta*
A. Ling; Heather	*Calluna vulgaris*
B. Pine	*Pinus picea*
C. Lucerne	*Trifolium rubens*
D. Oak	*Quercus pedunculata*

Plate 23
LIPARIDAE—BOMBYCOIDAE

Fig. 1, *a–c.*	*Leucoma salicis*
Fig. 2, *a–c.*	*Ocneria dispar*
Fig. 3.	*Ocneria monacha*
Fig. 4.	*Porthesia chrysorrhoea*
Fig. 5, *a, b.*	*Porthesia auriflua*
Fig. 6.	*Laria V.-nigra*
Fig. 7.	*Panthea coenobita*
A. Five-stamened Willow	*Salix pentandra*
B. Dog Rose	*Rosa rubrifolia*
C. Hornbeam	*Carpinus betulus*

Plate 24
COSSIDAE—COCHLIOPODIDAE—HEPIALIDAE—PSYCHIDAE

Fig. 1, *a–c.*	*Cossus ligniperda*
Fig. 2, *a, b.*	*Zeuzera aesculi*
Fig. 3.	*Limacodes testudo*
Fig. 4, *a, b.*	*Hepialus humuli*
Fig. 5.	*Hepialus lupulinus*
Fig. 6, *a, b.*	*Hepialus hectus*
Fig. 7, *a, b.*	*Psyche unicolor*
Fig. 8.	*Psyche viciella*
Fig. 9.	*Oreopsyche muscella*
A. Dandelion	*Leontodon taraxacum*
B. Sallow	*Salix caprea*
C. Apple	*Pyrus malus*

Plate 25
SATURNIIDAE

Fig. 1, *a–c.*	*Endromis versicolora*
Fig. 2, *a, b.*	*Saturnia pyri*
Fig. 3, *a–e.*	*Saturnia carpini*
A. Pear	*Pyrus communis*
B. Birch	*Betula alba*
C. Dog Rose	*Rosa canina*

Plate 26
LASIOCAMPIDAE

Fig. 1, *a–c.*	*Gastropacha quercifolia*
Fig. 2.	*Lasiocampa pruni*
Fig. 3, *a–c.*	*Lasiocampa pini*
Fig. 4, *a–c.*	*Lasiocampa potatoria*
Fig. 5.	*Clisiocampa populi*
Fig. 6, *a, b.*	*Clisiocampa neustria*
Fig. 7, *a–c.*	*Clisiocampa castrensis*
Fig. 8, *a, b.*	*Eriogaster catax*
A. Leafy-branched Spurge	*Euphorbia esula*
B. Plum	*Prunus domestica*
C. Scotch Fir	*Pinus sylvestris*

Plate 27
LASIOCAMPIDAE

Fig. 1, *a–e.*	*Lasiocampa quercus*
Fig. 2, *a–c.*	*Lasiocampa rubi*
Fig. 3, *a, b.*	*Eriogaster rimicola*
Fig. 4, *a, b.*	*Eriogaster lanestris*
Fig. 5.	*Crateronyx dumeti*
A. Sloe; Blackthorn	*Prunus spinosa*
B. Raspberry	*Rubus idaeus*
C. Oak	*Quercus robur*

Plate 28
DREPANULIDAE—NOTODONTIDAE

Fig. 1.	*Cilix glaucata*
Fig. 2.	*Drepana binaria*
Fig. 3.	*Platypteryx falcataria*
Fig. 4, *a–c.*	*Cerura vinula*
Fig. 5.	*Cerura erminea*
Fig. 6.	*Cerura bifida*
Fig. 7, *a, b.*	*Cerura hybocampa milhauseri*
Fig. 8, *a–c.*	*Stauropus fagi*
Fig. 9.	*Ptilophoro plumigera*
A. Oak	*Quercus pedunculata*
B. Osier	*Salix viminalis*
C. Hornbeam	*Carpinus betulus*

Plate 29
NOTODONTIDAE

Fig. 1.	*Phalera bucephala*
Fig. 2.	*Pterostoma palpina*
Fig. 3, *a, b.*	*Lophopteryx camelina*
Fig. 4.	*Odontosia carmelita*
Fig. 5.	*Microdonta bicolora*
Fig. 6.	*Leiocampa dictaea*
Fig. 7.	*Drymonia chaonia*
Fig. 8.	*Notodanta tritophus*
Fig. 9, *a–d.*	*Notodanta ziczac*
A. Willow	*Salix praecox*
B. Birch	*Betula alba*
C. Apple	*Pyrus malus*

Plate 30
CYMATOPHORIDAE—ACRONYCTIDAE

Fig. 1, *a, b.*	*Thyatira batis*
Fig. 2, *a, b.*	*Cymatophora or*

Fig. 3, *a, b.*	*Asphalia flavicornis*
Fig. 4, *a, b.*	*Asphalia ridens*
Fig. 5.	*Acronycta leporina*
Fig. 6, *a, b.*	*Acronycta alni*
Fig. 7, *a, b.*	*Acronycta psi*
Fig. 8.	*Acronycta aceris*
Fig. 9, *a, b.*	*Acronycta auricoma*
A. Bramble	*Rubus polymorphus*
B. Aspen	*Populus tremula*
C. Birch	*Betula alba*
D. Oak	*Quercus pedunculata*

Plate 31
BOMBYCOIDAE—ACRONYCTIDAE—ORTHOSIDAE

Fig. 1.	*Diphthera ludifica*
Fig. 2, *a, b.*	*Moma orion*
Fig. 3.	*Bryophila perla*
Fig. 4.	*Bryophila algae*
Fig. 5.	*Arsilonche albovenosa*
Fig. 6.	*Caradrina cubicularis*
Fig. 7.	*Asteroscopus sphinx*
Fig. 8, *a, b.*	*Panolis piniperda*
Fig. 9, *a, b.*	*Taeniocampa gothica*
Fig. 10.	*Taeniocampa stabilis*
Fig. 11.	*Orthosia rufina*
Fig. 12.	*Mesogona acetosellae*
Fig. 13.	*Cosmia affinis*
A. Oak	*Quercus robur*
B. Broom	*Sarothamnus scoparia*
C. Scotch Fir	*Pinus sylvestris*

Plate 32
ORTHOSIDAE

Fig. 1.	*Nonagria arundinis*
Fig. 2.	*Nonagria cannae*
Fig. 3, *a, b.*	*Leucania pallens*
Fig. 4.	*Leucania obsoleta*
Fig. 5, *a, b.*	*Gortyna flavago*
Fig. 6.	*Xanthia fulvago*
Fig. 7, *a, b.*	*Oporina croceago*
Fig. 8.	*Orrhodia rubiginea*
Fig. 9.	*Orrhodia vacinii*
Fig. 10, *a, b.*	*Mecoptera fragariae*
Fig. 11.	*Amphipyra pyramidea*
A. Red-berried Elder	*Sambucus racemosa*
B. Grass	
C. Wild Strawberry	*Fragaria fusca*
D. Oak	*Quercus robur*

Plate 33
AGROTIDAE

Fig. 1, *a–c.*	*Triphaena fimbria*
Fig. 2, *a, b.*	*Triphaena ianthina*
Fig. 3, *a, b.*	*Triphaena comes*
Fig. 4.	*Triphaena orbona*
Fig. 5, *a–c.*	*Triphaena pronuba*
Fig. 6.	*Hiria linogrisea*
A. Oxlip	*Primula officinalis*

B. Cuckoo-Pint   *Arum maculatum*
C. Red Lamium   *Lamium purpureum*

Plate 34
AGROTIDAE—HADENIDAE

Fig. 1.	*Agrotis festiva*
Fig. 2.	*Agrotis C.-nigrum*
Fig. 3.	*Agrotis sigma*
Fig. 4, *a, b.*	*Agrotis plecta*
Fig. 5.	*Agrotis putris*
Fig. 6.	*Agrotis praecox*
Fig. 7.	*Agrotis segetum*
Fig. 8, *a, b.*	*Mamestra persicariae*
Fig. 9, *a, b.*	*Mamestra brassicae*
Fig. 10.	*Mamestra nebulosa*
Fig. 11.	*Mamestra tincta*
Fig. 12, *a, b.*	*Mamestra leucophaea*
A. Wild Cabbage	*Brassica oleracea*
B. Wild Cherry	*Cichorium intybus*
C. Common Rose Persicaria	*Polygonum persicaria*

Plate 35
ORTHOSIDAE—HADENIDAE

Fig. 1.	*Luperina virens*
Fig. 2.	*Miselia oxyacanthae*
Fig. 3, *a, b.*	*Dichonia aprilina*
Fig. 4.	*Polia chi*
Fig. 5, *a–c.*	*Dianthoecia albimacula*
Fig. 6, *a–c.*	*Dianthoecia compta*
Fig. 7, *a, b.*	*Mamestra dysodea*
Fig. 8.	*Mamestra dentina*
Fig. 9.	*Mamestra oleracea*
Fig. 10, *a, b.*	*Mamestra pisi*
Fig. 11.	*Hadena monoglypha*
A. Meadow Vetchling	*Lathyrus pratensis*
B. Wild Carnation	*Dianthus carthusianorum*
C. Lettuce	*Lactuca sativa*
D. Bladder Campion	*Silene inflata*
E. Oak	*Quercus pedunculata*

Plate 36
HADENIDAE—XYLINIDAE

Fig. 1, *a, b.*	*Valeria oleagina*
Fig. 2.	*Chariptera culta*
Fig. 3.	*Hadena didyma*
Fig. 4.	*Hadena strigilis*
Fig. 5.	*Dipterygia pinastri*
Fig. 6.	*Euplexia lucipara*
Fig. 7, *a, b.*	*Habryntis suta*
Fig. 8.	*Habryntis meticulosa*
Fig. 9.	*Rhizogramma detersa*
Fig. 10.	*Ercopus purpureofasciatus*
Fig. 11.	*Xylinia ornithopus*
Fig. 12, *a, b.*	*Calocampa exoleta*
Fig. 13.	*Xylomyges conspicillaris*
A. Sloe; Blackthorn	*Prunus spinosa*
B. Vetch	*Pisum arvense*
C. Grass	
D. Sweet Violet	*Viola odorata*

Plate 37
ORTHOSIDAE—CLEOPHANIDAE—CUCULLIDAE—HELIOTHIDAE—
ANARTIDAE—ACONTIDAE

Fig. 1.	*Scoliopteryx libatrix*
Fig. 2.	*Calophasia lunula*
Fig. 3, *a–c.*	*Cucullia verbasci*
Fig. 4.	*Cucullia umbratica*
Fig. 5, *a, b.*	*Cucullia lactucae*
Fig. 6, *a–c.*	*Cucullia argentea*
Fig. 7.	*Heliothis dipsacea*
Fig. 8.	*Chariclea delphinii*
Fig. 9.	*Heliaca tenebrata*
Fig. 10.	*Abrostola triplasia*
Fig. 11.	*Acontia luctuosa*
A. Lettuce	*Lactuca sativa*
B. Mullein	*Verbascum thapsus*
C. Field Southernwood	*Artemisia campestris*

Plate 38
PLUSIDAE—OPHIUSIDAE—TOXOCAMPIDAE

Fig. 1.	*Plusia bractea*
Fig. 2.	*Plusia iota*
Fig. 3, *a, b.*	*Plusia gamma*
Fig. 4.	*Plusia hochenwarthi*
Fig. 5.	*Euclidia glyphica*
Fig. 6.	*Euclidia mi*
Fig. 7.	*Pseudophia tirrhaea*
Fig. 8, *a–c.*	*Pseudophia lunaris*
Fig. 9, *a, b.*	*Toxocampa lusoria*
Fig. 10.	*Toxocampa craccae*
A. Tufted Vetch	*Vicia cracca*
B. Yellow Lamium	*Galeobdolon luteum*
C. Oak	*Quercus pedunculata*

Plate 39
HADENIDAE—OPHIUSIDAE—BREPHIDAE

Fig. 1.	*Mormo maura*
Fig. 2.	*Catephia alchymista*
Fig. 3, *a, b.*	*Catocala fraxini*
Fig. 4.	*Catocala nupta*
Fig. 5, *a, b.*	*Catocala sponsa*
Fig. 6.	*Catocala electa*
Fig. 7, *a, b.*	*Catocala paranympha*
Fig. 8.	*Brephos parthenias*
A. Oak	*Quercus pedunculata*
B. Osier	*Salix viminalis*
C. Sloe; Blackthorn	*Prunus spinosa*

Plate 40
NOCTUOPHALAENIDAE—DELTOIDAE—CHLOEPHORIDAE

Fig. 1.	*Erastria deceptoria*
Fig. 2.	*Erastria fasciana*
Fig. 3, *a, b.*	*Emmelia trabealis*
Fig. 4.	*Trothisa respersa*
Fig. 5.	*Trothisa rosea*
Fig. 6.	*Trothisa purpurina*
Fig. 7.	*Herminia tentacularia*
Fig. 8.	*Herminia derivalis*
Fig. 9, *a–d.*	*Halias prasinana*

Fig. 10, *a–d.*	*Chloephora bicolorana*
A. Beech	*Fagus sylvatica*
B. Small Bindweed	*Convolvulus arvensis*
C. Oak	*Quercus pedunculata*

Plate 41
DENDROMETRIDAE

Fig. 1, *a, b.*	*Metrocampa margaritaria*
Fig. 2, *a–c.*	*Eugonia autumnaria*
Fig. 3, *a–c.*	*Selenia tetralunaria*
Fig. 4, *a–c.*	*Himeria pennaria*
Fig. 5.	*Macaria notata*
Fig. 6.	*Urapteryx sambucaria*
Fig. 7, *a–c.*	*Amphidasis betularia*
A. Alder	*Almus glutinosa*
B. Birch	*Betula alba*
C. Gooseberry	*Ribes grossularia*
D. Beech	*Fagus sylvatica*

Plate 42
DENDROMETRIDAE

Fig. 1, *a, b.*	*Selenia bilunaria*
Fig. 2, *a, b.*	*Rumia crataegata*
Fig. 3, *a–d.*	*Angerona prunaria*
Fig. 4.	*Hibernia defoliaria*
Fig. 5.	*Hibernia aurantiaria*
Fig. 6.	*Hibernia leucophaearia*
Fig. 7.	*Timandra amataria*
A. Hawthorn	*Crataegus oxyacantha*
B. Broom	*Sarothamnus scoparia*
C. Sloe; Blackthorn	*Prunus spinosa*

Plate 43
DENDROMETRIDAE

Fig. 1.	*Venilia macularia*
Fig. 2.	*Bapta bimaculata*
Fig. 3.	*Abraxas sylvata*
Fig. 4.	*Abraxas pantaria*
Fig. 5, *a–d.*	*Abraxas grossulariata*
Fig. 6, *a–c.*	*Abraxas marginata*
Fig. 7.	*Rhyparia melanaria*
Fig. 8, *a, b.*	*Fidonia piniaria*
Fig. 9.	*Fidonia atomaria*
Fig. 10.	*Thamnonoma wavaria*
Fig. 11.	*Fidoniae clathrata*
A. Red Currant	*Ribes rubrum*
B. Hazel	*Corylus avellana*

Plate 44
DENDROMETRIDAE

Fig. 1.	*Cabera exanthemata*
Fig. 2.	*Boarmia cinctaria*
Fig. 3.	*Boarmia secundaria*
Fig. 4.	*Boarmia consortaria*
Fig. 5, *a–c.*	*Boarmia roboraria*
Fig. 6.	*Boarmia crepuscularia*
Fig. 7.	*Biston strataria*
Fig. 8, *a–c.*	*Biston hirtaria*
Fig. 9, *a, b.*	*Biston pilosaria*

Fig. 10.	*Biston pomonaria*
Fig. 11.	*Biston zonaria*
A. Oak	*Quercus robur*
B. Hawthorn	*Crataegus oxyacantha*
C. Alder	*Alnus incana*

Plate 45
DENDROMETRIDAE—PHYTOMETRIDAE

Fig. 1.	*Psodos quadrifaria*
Fig. 2, *a, b.*	*Pseudoterpna pruinata*
Fig. 3.	*Geometra papilionaria*
Fig. 4, *a–c.*	*Phorodesma smaragdaria*
Fig. 5.	*Nemoria vernaria*
Fig. 6.	*Acidalia humiliata*
Fig. 7, *a, b.*	*Acidalia virgularia*
Fig. 8.	*Acidalia aversata*
Fig. 9.	*Acidalia emarginata*
Fig. 10.	*Acidalia immutata*
Fig. 11.	*Pellonia vibicaria*
Fig. 12.	*Zonosoma trilinearia*
Fig. 13.	*Anisopteryx aescularia*
Fig. 14.	*Minoa murinata*
Fig. 15.	*Lythria purpuraria*
Fig. 16.	*Eupithecia rectangulata*
A. Buckthorn	*Rhamnus frangula*
B.	*Cytisus nigricans*
C. Yarrow	*Achillea millefolium*

Plate 46
PHYTOMETRIDAE

Fig. 1.	*Ortholitha palumbaria*
Fig. 2.	*Ortholitha bipunctaria*
Fig. 3, *a–c.*	*Scotosa certata*
Fig. 4.	*Scotosa undulata*
Fig. 5.	*Larentia fluctuata*
Fig. 6.	*Larentia bilineata*
Fig. 7.	*Larentia tristata*
Fig. 8.	*Larentia hastata*
Fig. 9, *a–c.*	*Larentia derivata*
Fig. 10.	*Larentia berberata*
Fig. 11.	*Larentia fulvata*
Fig. 12.	*Larentia viridaria*
Fig. 13, *a, b.*	*Oporabia dilutata*
Fig. 14, *a, b.*	*Cheimatobia brumata*
A. Barberry	*Berberis vulgaris*
B. Elm	*Ulmus effusa*
C. Dog Rose	*Rosa canina*

Plate 47
DENDROMETRIDAE

Fig. 1, *a, b.*	*Therapis evonymaria*
Fig. 2, *a, b.*	*Pericallia syringaria*
Fig. 3, *a, b.*	*Crocallis elinguaria*
Fig. 4, *a, b.*	*Eurymene dolabraria*
Fig. 5.	*Epione advenaria*
Fig. 6.	*Epione apiciaria*
Fig. 7.	*Diastictis artesiaria*
Fig. 8.	*Ploseria diversata*
Fig. 9.	*Scoria lineata*
Fig. 10.	*Phasiane petraria*

A. Honeysuckle	*Lonicera xylosteum*
B. Spindle Tree	*Evonymus europaeus*
C. Oak	*Quercus robur*

Plate 48
DENDROMETRIDAE—PHYTOMETRIDAE

Fig. 1.	*Odontopera bidentata*
Fig. 2, *a, b.*	*Hypoplectis adspersaria*
Fig. 3.	*Aspilates gilvaria*
Fig. 4.	*Numeria pulveraria*
Fig. 5.	*Gnophos dilucidaria*
Fig. 6.	*Tephronia sepiaria*
Fig. 7.	*Pachycnemia hippocastanaria*
Fig. 8.	*Nemoria fimbrialis*
Fig. 9.	*Nemoria porrinata*
Fig. 10.	*Odezia atrata*
Fig. 11.	*Anaitis plagiata*
Fig. 12, *a, b.*	*Chesias spartiata*
Fig. 13.	*Chesias farinata*
Fig. 14.	*Lobophora sexalisata*
Fig. 15, *a, b.*	*Larentia albicillata*
A. Broom	*Sarothamnus scoparia*
B. Raspberry	*Rubus idaeus*
C. Bird's-foot Trefoil	*Lotus corniculatus*

Plate 49
RHOPALOCERA

Fig. 1.	*Thais cerisyi*
Fig. 2.	*Genepteryx cleopatra*
Fig. 3.	*Euchloe belemia*
Fig. 4, *a, b.*	*Zegris eupheme*
Fig. 5.	*Argynnis laodice*
Fig. 6.	*Vanessa levana*
Fig. 7.	*Vanessa ichnusa*
Fig. 8.	*Spilothyrus lavaterae*
Fig. 9.	*Pamphila nostrodamus*
Fig. 10, *a, b.*	*Gonepteryx rhamni* (larva and pupa)
A. Buckthorn	*Rhamnus frangula*
B.	*Sinapis incana*

Plate 50
RHOPALOCERA

Fig. 1.	*Satyrus roxelana*
Fig. 2.	*Oeneis aëllo*
Fig. 3, *a, b.*	*Satyrus achine*
Fig. 4, *a, b.*	*Triphysa phryne*
Fig. 5.	*Caenonympha oedipus*
Fig. 6, *a, b.*	*Epinephile lycaon*
Fig. 7.	*Caenonympha hero*
Fig. 8.	*Polyommatus orion*
Fig. 9.	*Polyommatus pheretes*
Fig. 10.	*Polyommatus cyllarus*
Fig. 11.	*Polyommatus damon*
Fig. 12.	*Polyommatus baeticus*
Fig. 13.	*Laeosopis roboris*
Fig. 14.	*Thestor ballus*
A. Grass	
B. Rye-grass	*Lolium perenne*
C. Grass	

Plate 51
BOMBYCES

Fig. 1, *a–c.*	*Actias isabellae*
Fig. 2.	*Lasiocampa otus*
Fig. 3.	*Euprepia pudica*
Fig. 4.	*Saturnia caecigena*
Fig. 5.	*Endagria pantherina*
Fig. 6.	*Stygia australis*
Fig. 7.	*Naclia ancilla*
A. Pineaster	*Pinus maritima*

Plate 52
NOCTUAE

Fig. 1.	*Gonophora derasa*
Fig. 2.	*Dasypolia templi*
Fig. 3.	*Pachnobia carnea*
Fig. 4.	*Episema trimacula*
Fig. 5.	*Clidia chamaesyces*
Fig. 6.	*Tapinostola bondii*
Fig. 7.	*Stilbia anomala*
Fig. 8, *a–c.*	*Brithys pancratii*
Fig. 9.	*Eogena contaminei*
Fig. 10, *a, b.*	*Raphia hybris*
Fig. 11.	*Acosmetia caleginosa*
Fig. 12.	*Arsilonche albovenosa*
A. Black Poplar	*Populus nigra*
B.	*Pancratium maritimum*

Plate 53
NOCTUAE

Fig. 1.	*Dianthoecia capsophila*
Fig. 2.	*Polyphaenis sericata*
Fig. 3.	*Cleophana anarrhini*
Fig. 4.	*Miselia bimaculosa*
Fig. 5.	*Jaspidea celsia*
Fig. 6.	*Dianthoecia caesia*
Fig. 7.	*Oncocnemis confusa*
Fig. 8.	*Dianthoecia luteago*
Fig. 9.	*Hiptelia ochreago*
Fig. 10.	*Prodenia littoralis*
Fig. 11.	*Valeria jaspidea*
Fig. 12, *a, b.*	*Ulochlaena hirta*
A. Grass	

Plate 54
NOCTUAE

Fig. 1.	*Anthoecia cardui*
Fig. 2.	*Hadena exulis,* variety *Assimilis*
Fig. 3.	*Heliodes theophila*
Fig. 4.	*Hadena sommeri*
Fig. 5.	*Omia cymbalariae*
Fig. 6.	*Anarta myrtilli*
Fig. 7, *a, b.*	*Eurhipia adulatrix*
Fig. 8.	*Xanthodes malvae*
Fig. 9, *a, b.*	*Xanthodes graëllsii*
Fig. 10, *a, b.*	*Hadena exulis*
A.	*Pistacia lentiscus*
B. Mallow	*Lavatera*
C. Grass	

Plate 55
NOCTUAE

Fig. 1.	*Zethes insularis*
Fig. 2.	*Calpe capucina*
Fig. 3.	*Ophiusa algira*
Fig. 4.	*Telesilla amethystina*
Fig. 5.	*Prothymia viridaria*
Fig. 6.	*Ophiusa cailino*
Fig. 7.	*Haemerosia renalis*
Fig. 8.	*Anophia funesta*
Fig. 9.	*Pseudophia illunaris*
Fig. 10, *a, b.*	*Anophia leucomelas*
Fig. 11, *a, b.*	*Cerocala scapulosa*
A. Larger Convolvulus	*Convolvulus sepium*
B. Cistus	*Helianthemum halimifolium*

Plate 56
NOCTUAE—NYCTEOLIDAE

Fig. 1.	*Spintherops spectrum*
Fig. 2.	*Metoptria monogramma*
Fig. 3.	*Aventia flexula*
Fig. 4.	*Boletobia fuliginaria*
Fig. 5, *a, b.*	*Ophiusa bifasciata*
Fig. 6.	*Nola togatulalis*
Fig. 7.	*Metoponia agatha*
Fig. 8.	*Bomolocha fontis*
Fig. 9.	*Paidia mesogona*
Fig. 10.	*Hypena rostralis*
Fig. 11.	*Zanclognatha tarsipennalis*
Fig. 12.	*Madopa salicalis*
Fig. 13, *a, b.*	*Alamis albidens*
A.	*Polygonum rosmarinum*
B. Whin	*Genista*

Plate 57
GEOMETRAE

Fig. 1.	*Thamnonoma vincularia*
Fig. 2.	*Collix sparsaria*
Fig. 3.	*Selidosema plumeria*
Fig. 4.	*Aplasta ononaria*
Fig. 5.	*Sterrha sacraria*
Fig. 6.	*Sparta paradoxaria*
Fig. 7.	*Orthostixis cribraria*
Fig. 8.	*Proplepsis ocellata*
Fig. 9.	*Terpnomicta trimaculata*
Fig. 10.	*Siona decussata*
Fig. 11.	*Fidonia plumistaria*
Fig. 12, *a, b.*	*Eucrostis indigenata*
A. Spurge	*Euphorba spinosa*

Plate 58
GEOMETRAE

Fig. 1.	*Cleogene peletieraria*
Fig. 2.	*Gnophos obfuscata*
Fig. 3.	*Scodiona belgaria*
Fig. 4.	*Cimelia margarita*
Fig. 5.	*Pygmaena fusca*

Fig. 6.	*Eusarca badiaria*
Fig. 7.	*Nychiodes lividaria*
Fig. 8.	*Hemerophila abruptaria*
Fig. 9.	*Eilicrinia cordiariae*
Fig. 10.	*Ligia opacaria*
Fig. 11, *a, b.*	*Chemerina caliginearia*
A. Cistus	*Helianthemum*

Plate 59
PYRALES—TORTRICES

Fig. 1, *a, b.*	*Hydrocampa nymphaeata*
Fig. 2, *a, b.*	*Odontia dentalis*
Fig. 3.	*Ennychia nigrata*
Fig. 4.	*Threnodes pollinalis*
Fig. 5.	*Pyrausta purpuralis*
Fig. 6, *a, b.*	*Botys urticata*
Fig. 7.	*Botys flavalis*
Fig. 8.	*Botys hyalinalis*
Fig. 9.	*Crambus selasellus*
Fig. 10.	*Crambus pinetellus*
Fig. 11, *a, b.*	*Pempelia semirubella*
Fig. 12, *a–c.*	*Myelophila cribrum*
Fig. 13.	*Galleria mellonella*
Fig. 14.	*Aglossa pinguinalis*
Fig. 15.	*Pyralis farinalis*
Fig. 16.	*Teras caudana*
Fig. 17.	*Lozotaenia sorbiana*
Fig. 18, *a, b.*	*Tortrix viridana*
A. Water Lily	*Nymphaea*
B. Viper's Bugloss	*Echium vulgare*
C. Dog Rose	*Rosa canina*
D. Clover	*Trifolium*
E. Nettle	*Urtica dioica*
F. Oak	*Quercus robur*

Plate 60
TORTRICES—TINEAE—PTEROPHORI

Fig. 1.	*Penthina salicella*
Fig. 2, *a, b.*	*Retinia resinella*
Fig. 3.	*Antithesia pruniana*
Fig. 4.	*Grapholitha citrana*
Fig. 5, *a, b.*	*Carpocapsa pomonella*
Fig. 6.	*Tinea tapetzella*
Fig. 7.	*Euplocamus anthracinalis*
Fig. 8.	*Incurvaria muscalella*
Fig. 9.	*Nemophora swammerdammella*
Fig. 10.	*Adela degeerella*
Fig. 11.	*Cerostoma dentella*
Fig. 12.	*Hyponomeuta evonymella*
Fig. 13, *a, b.*	*Hyponomeuta cognatella*
Fig. 14.	*Chimabacche fagella*
Fig. 15.	*Psecadia pusiella*
Fig. 16.	*Psecadia bipunctella*
Fig. 17.	*Pterophorus pterodactylus*
Fig. 18.	*Pterophorus carphodactylus*
Fig. 19.	*Pterophorus pentadactylus*
A. Scotch Fir	*Pinus sylvestris*
B. Spindle Tree	*Evonymus europaeus*
C. Apple	*Pyrus malus*

ALPHABETICAL INDEX OF LATIN NAMES

71